D1566479

drawing the line

POEMS BY LAWSON FUSAO INADA

drawing the line

COFFEE HOUSE PRESS • MINNEAPOLIS • 1997

Photograph in the introduction by Masako Inada, from *In This Great Land of Freedom,* Japanese American National Museum, 1993. Cover art by Yosh Kuromiya. Cover design by Jinger Peissig. Back cover photograph by Bill McClain.

The author thanks the editors of the following publications, where many of these poems first appeared: *Ergo!; Homeground; Many Mountains Moving; Premonitions; The Pushcart Prize* XIX; *Tricycle;* a version of "Ringing the Bell" appeared in *Edge Walking on the Western Rim;* "This One, That One" appeared in a chapbook, *Just Intonations,* with sumi-e art by Robert Kostka; "Picture" was inspired by a painting by Betty LaDuke; "Seeking the Great" owes thanks to Tom Ferté, editor of *Calapooya Collage.*

Coffee House Press is supported in part by a grant provided by the Minnesota State Arts Board, through an appropriation by the Minnesota State Legislature, and by a grant from the National Endowment for the Arts, a federal agency. Additional support has been provided by the The McKnight Foundation; Lannan Foundation; Jerome Foundation; Lila Wallace-Reader's Digest Fund; Target Stores, Dayton's, and Mervyn's by the Dayton Hudson Foundation; General Mills Foundation; St. Paul Companies; Honeywell Foundation; Star Tribune/Cowles Media Company; The Butler Family Foundation; The James R. Thorpe Foundation; Dain Bosworth Foundation; The Beverly J. and John A. Rollwagen Fund of The Minneapolis Foundation; and The Andrew W. Mellon Foundation.

Coffee House Press books are available to the trade through our primary distributor, Consortium Book Sales & Distribution, 1045 Westgate Drive, Saint Paul, MN 55114. For personal orders, catalogs, or other information, write to: Coffee House Press, 27 North Fourth Street, Suite 400, Minneapolis, MN 55401.

Library of Congress CIP Data
  Drawing the line: poems / by Lawson Fusao Inada
    p.   cm.
  ISBN 1-56689-060-8 (alk. paper)
PS3559.N3D731997
811'.54—dc21

PS
3559
.N3
D73
1997

96-53370

CIP

10   9   8   7   6   5   4   3   2   1

72600

Contents

I. JUST AS I THOUGHT

7 Just As I Thought
13 This One, That One
17 Over Here, Over There

II. THE REAL INADA

31 The Real Inada
39 Denver Union Station
42 The Grand Silos of the Sacramento
43 Grandmother
44 Eatin' with Sticks
47 In a Buddhist Forest
48 Kicking the Habit

III. RINGING THE BELL

55 Ringing the Bell
59 The Real Fresno
61 Residue
63 Messing with the Sisters
64 Nobody, Nothing
67 Hiroshi from Hiroshima
86 A Nice Place

IV. PUTTING BACK THE RAIN

89 Putting Back the Rain
90 Pursuing a Career
93 A World of Passengers
94 A High-Five for I-5

100 Seeking the Great
102 Picture
104 Tapping the Temples

V. DRAWING THE LINE

109 A Poet of the High Seas
110 Healing Gila
112 Children of Camp
117 Scanning the Century
124 Picking Up Stones
128 Drawing the Line

Dedication

Dr. Fusaji Inada, D.D.S.
1910-1996

Consider the qualities
You most admire
In an elder

And be blessed
With the presence
Of my father.

INTRODUCTION

Miju Murakami Inada, Lawson Fusao Inada
Fresno, California, ca. 1941

I.

Here is a picture of an Issei woman. What do you suppose she is thinking and feeling? Obviously, she is thinking about her grandson, and feeling joy, and love. She is also feeling the warmth of the sun, while enjoying a rare day off from her labors on the farm.

She can look back at her life with pride and satisfaction. Born and raised in a Japanese village, she came to America in 1901, joining her husband who had labored there since 1896. They became sharecroppers, moving from farm to farm with other pioneer families, making history and communities along the way.

Hers was a grueling, fulfilling life, full of struggle, sacrifice, celebration, and wonder. She served as fieldhand, healer, community counselor, always counted on to hold things together. She could make soup from rain, beauty from scrap; she made everything feel special with her appreciation and grace. The land was beautiful, the harvests plentiful. What more to ask?

Thus, today, she feels happy, blessed. Within a year, she would be dead and her grandson, Lawson, in a concentration camp.

II.

Everything in here goes right back to there: 705 E Street, corner of Mono, West Fresno. My ancestry, for instance: my Inada grandmother visiting my Saito grandparents.

Or look at the direction I'm heading: across Mono to the Hernandez home and the music of Veracruz (see "A Poet of the High Seas"). And after the war, the Jones family moved into that house (see "Ringing the Bell").

Everything was there, in place, and has stayed with me since.

And if I kept going one block on E, I'd be at the corner of Ventura, could turn left, stroll a ways, and arrive early at the site of our initial camp, the Fresno County Fairgrounds.

Or, if I went in the other direction on E, I'd be at the Buddhist temple in a minute. And at the edge of the business district known as Chinatown—so named for its founders, but the place of commerce for people of African, Asian, Latin American, and American Indian ancestry, as well as Armenians, Basques, Germans, Greeks, Irish, Italians, Jews, Okies . . .

My feet, in a matter of feet, could take me all over the world—and I went.

III.

It was a world of "across," "down," "around." And that house, that yard, was pretty much "Japan," naturally, while simultaneously being, of course, "Anywhere, u.s.a.," inhabited by the American athletes and scholars and servicemen who were my uncles.

And since it was my grandparents' home, it was also the headquarters for one of West Fresno's, Fresno's, and the valley's major cultural institutions, the Fresno Fish Market, the first in all the region, founded in 1912.

So there I was, in 1941 . . .

IV.

It's all gone now. After my grandparents passed, the house was sold to members of the Palomino family (also see "Ringing the Bell") before being bulldozed by industry.

But appearances can be deceiving. I could stand there right now, on the asphalt of that massive area, on the bank of and in the clamor of what became the four-lane Highway 99 freeway, and what would come to me would be the fragrance of food, the waves of music, and, most certainly, the presence of people. . . .

And, once again, I would be immersed in, surrounded by, all that culture, history, tradition—and as I toddled off in the direction of poetry, Grandma would smile and say: "Ah, yes—we came to America for that!"

I

just as i thought

JUST AS I THOUGHT

Just as I thought: One blue jay
                      shakes
                      a whole morning.

Just as I thought: The streetsweeper
                      is related
                      to the preacher.

Just as I thought: Big orange berries
                      on a bush;
                      small green apples
                      on a tree;
                      bright blue sky
                      in between:

                      Even a non-goat
                      can be happy.

Just as I thought: We feel
                      nostalgia
                      for life
                      before
                      karma.

Just as I thought: This is the same old water.

Just as I thought: Like a pond,
                      I respond.

Just as I thought: A river
                      A prayer.
                      Skipping stones.

Just as I thought: No two are the same.

Just as I thought: That distant train,
this train of thought . . .

Just as I thought: According to turtles,
rivers are a fluid
form of bridges.

Just as I thought: Anywhere we go,
we hear buffalo.

Just as I thought: The magnificent value
of that plastic chair
accrues each and every
time I randomly move
it to a distinctively
new location of lawn.

Just as I thought: Plus, go right ahead—
toss it, tip it, kick it,
bite it—no problema.

Just as I thought: Plus, you oughta
see it in moonlight
with a smooth she-
feline in it.

Just as I thought: Plus, since it's ivory,
it makes quite a sight
when a necktied man
rears back in that baby
in broad daylight,
with a cup of coffee,
and makes him a couple
of long-distance calls.

Just as I thought: Leaves gather in it.

Just as I thought: Nope, I don't have nothing,
not Word One, please,
to say about leaves.

Just as I thought: Clouds, neither.
Absolutely not!
Do you hear me?

Just as I thought: After several tries,
I still can't finish,
with a straight face,
"I despise . . ."

Just as I thought: Hail-slash-sun,
cold-slash-warm,
being-slash-being.

Just as I thought: If I had a piano,
I'd make rain.

Just as I thought: Marimba Zimbabwe!

Just as I thought: My politics revolves
around the sun.

Just as I thought: Tornados are sky
mating with earth.

Just as I thought: Rows of fenced
storage units:
Back in camp.

Just as I thought: Who drew a red
mustache on the white
man on my money?

Just as I thought: Dust doesn't discriminate.

Just as I thought: "Over here!"
                     whispers
                     the mirror.

Just as I thought: Blue jay's shadow
                     weighs a lot more
                     than I thought.

Just as I thought: Your wind chimes remind me.

Just as I thought: Although you are
                     not the same fly
                     I released last
                     week from the car—

                     we are reunited,
                     parent and child.

Just as I thought: "I'm off!" mocks the clock.

Just as I thought: Blue jay on the roof
                     stomps out apostrophes.

Just as I thought: Out of respect,
                     and to be correct
                     when you pray,
                     make the old sign
                     of quotation marks.

Just as I thought: Few is always more
                     than less.

Just as I thought: Recorded music
                     is composed
                     of fossils.

Just as I thought: When the moon is full
                     is when it is hollow.

Just as I thought: My sleepy mind holds,
                     but just barely,
                     from side to side,
                     top to bottom,
                     a fully grown,
                     loaded with cones,
                     swaying and shiny-
                     needled pine tree.

Just as I thought: Blue jay dreams
                     green jay dreams . . .

Just as I thought: Coyotes and toenails.

Just as I thought: Or, war, wind, hollows . . .

Just as I thought: The green hose
                     sprawls where
                     I left it being
                     calligraphy,
                     a new art form;

                     tomorrow, I'll
                     rearrange it,
                     respecting its
                     connections
                     to its factory
                     in Singapore.

Just as I thought: What *isn't* a fragment?

Just as I thought: Body of water,
                     body of mind,
                     floating . . .

Just as I thought: Ah, where have you been,
                    rain? "Guess . . ."

Just as I thought: Thought I as just.

Just as I thought: Acorns
                    Fall
                    What
                    Did
                    They
                    Call

This One, That One

This one appeared to me
in a dream, was forgotten,
only to reveal itself
on the shower wall
this morning.
It must have been the water.

 *

That one was on the full moon
last night, clear as a bell.
Someone projected it there.

 *

This one was on the ground,
on crunchy pine needles.
The moon projected it there.

 *

I forgot about that one . . .
How was I to know
it would be significant?

 *

Every time I see this one,
I'm angry. It doesn't diminish,
either, from that first time.

 *

Oh, that one!
To tell you the truth,
I never actually
saw it, but I could
feel it as it was
described to me
by a blind person
over the phone.

*

This one I spotted
on the back
of someone's shirt
in a crowd
before she disappeared.

*

That one evolved,
and is still evolving,
on that big, flat rock
over there; something
scraped it, scratched it,
the heat cracked it,
the frost coated it,
tiny plants took root,
sheltering insects,
and it rained,
and it rained,
and by the time
I showed up,
a butterfly had just flown off.

*

Not this one again.
It makes me so sad . . .

*

I was glad to receive
that one as a gift.
So glad, in fact,
that I went and had
some copies made.

*

Believe it or not,
this one has a sound.
Just listen.

*

Oh, boy—that one!
I'll never go there again.

*

This one often arrives
in the smoke of incense.

*

I tried to turn
that one over—
it burned my hand.

*

This one I tried
to discard—
unsuccessfully, obviously.

*

That one speaks to me
of space, and negative space,
of open and filled spaces,
and the among
that comes between.

*

Whereas this one
is the opposite—
you get the picture.

*

Oh, my goodness—
I've never seen
that one before!

*

This one, from what
I gather,
is an accident.

*

That one, however,
is intended.

*

This one took some
getting to—
waiting for the thaw,
for instance—
but it was
well worth it.

*

That one, well,
you can have it.

*

Whenever this one
comes my way,
it's déjà vu,
but I'm ready for it.

*

That one is owned
by the dentist.

*

This one has been
proven to be a fake,
but I still like it.

*

Alas, I lost
that one once,
in childhood,
and it took me
until now to find it.

*

If you can only have
one, choose this one.

OVER HERE, OVER THERE

Over here,
you get
the full
effect.

> *Over there,*
> you miss it
> entirely.

Over here, see, is where
that sharp screwdriver
caught my brow, and,
instead of gouging
out my right eye,
went right up into
my forehead, to where
the scar is now,

faded a bit, with time,
but at the time
enabling me to learn
not to hurry,
not to create
my own fix,
and certainly
not to further
worry my mother

who already had
her hands full
with packing, panic,
filling crates,

and didn't need
to deal with doctors,
prayers, stitches,
bandages for weeks;

yes, instead,
I should have simply
sat down on the rolled-
up rug and trusted
in my father to come
home from lunch
and take matters
in his own grown hands
to fix the wagon
which wasn't going
anywhere anyway.

But we certainly were,
for shortly, quickly,
slowly, soon, thereafter,
in my immediate mind,
I was patiently able
to manage to observe,
bandage and all,
in our own sweet time,
an entire panorama
behind barbed wire,
with my own two eyes.

          "Over There." We would sing
          that over and over—
          "Over there. Over there."—
          over there in grammar school,
          which isn't there
          anymore, alas, gone
          with grammar, grammarians,

and the Great War,
during which the Yanks
did things
over there, like
"pass the ammunition,"
before coming

over here
in parades
of patrol cars
looking for trouble
and disturbing the peace;

and the thing about
the Yanks was—
even should you
manage to
grow up,
even should you
manage to move
over there,
and even should you
somehow manage to
even join them—

you could never
become one.

I had an itch
back *over here*
I couldn't quite reach;
it was specifically
in the notch
of my left shoulder blade
and, since I was single

(or "unattached")
at the time, I had to go
through contortions to reach
that part of myself
I'm not so sure
I've ever really seen
(nor really gotten to know,
like my chest);
and why my *left*
shoulder blade?
I would ask,
"how about some place
more convenient, man?"
and the itch, looking back,
didn't have much
of an answer,
since it wasn't
anything for a doctor
to deal with, not really
anything to show or see,
but it was more like
something had, as they
used to say, gotten
"under my skin"
like a desire, a wish,
a hankering, a downright
desperate need
requiring a breakthrough,
a breakout,
that was not simply
to be soothed
on the surface;
so the itch would come
and go, mostly come
and stay, and so I got

used to it, like a hum,
persistent, insistent,
out of reach,
out of hand,
but never quite
out of mind
even after a hot shower
with a scrubby brush,
a scratchy towel,
a cool and bracing
splash of alcohol, as
it finally occurred to me
that, rather than
seeking out some savanna
to rub against a tree,
the convenient thing
would be to confront
what needed facing;
and so I backed
into marriage, backed
into becoming
a parent, and the itch
apparently agreed
to spread all over,
to where it keeps me
tickled all the time.

      You may have to use
      your imagination, but way
      over there, way under
      all that rippling
      reservoir water, about
      in the middle, where
      the full moon
      is floating now,

is an early
spring morning,
a winding road,
and a rapid river

where a father
took his son
for a daylong
lesson in

skills, patience, vision, perseverance, tools,
pools, shadows, insects, depth, foam, trembling,
perceptions, heat, dew, fluids, pebbles, echoes,
boulders, breezes, respect, predecessors, sweat,
weight, muscles, glare, lizards, lunch, silence,
birds, conversation, snakes, space, naps, presence,

and how rainbows
really have to do
with moments
of memory, and peace,
as right here and now.

Over here, not far
from my family,
I was surprised
to find a friend
they didn't know,
Christopher, buried.

Right *over there,* obviously,
on my very property, obviously,
and despite whatever obvious
measures I take, obviously,
to keep things under control—

secured, symmetrical, neat—
as you can see now,
as you can *feel* now,
year after year after year
appear those noisy, invasive,
pushy, shovy, nosy, obtrusive,
intrusive, lazy, mocking,
mooching, show-offy, obviously
obvious pride-of-my-yard sunflowers!

And then *over here*—
careful, now, for that
trip wire, the orange
glaze, the scorched
spots, not to mention
the expected briars
and tangling vines—
is my transplanted
stand of Asian berries.

It was a simple enough game—
So simple, in fact, that
You surely know what I mean;
I'd guess my grandparents
Played it in their language,
So I'd assume it's universal,
Since it simply involves
Moving from *over there* to
Over here, or vice versa;
Perhaps it's even "tribal,"
With origins arching back
To fire, archetypal rituals
Regarding harvest, conflict,
Territory, mating, death,
With actual ramifications

And a real price to pay;
But we were just playing;
Heck, we didn't even know
We were chanting, evoking,
Summoning, challenging,
Tampering, taking risk;
We were simply trying to do
Something fun around dusk,
Being unruly within rules,
Unreasonable within reason,
Chasing, grabbing, catching,
Being dramatic on purpose,
And although I still don't
Know who Red Rover is,
We sense it in all of us,
And it always is the same.

Over here,
X marks
the spot;

now it's
your turn,
with the

"O!"

I was sitting right
over there, on the back steps
of the old Armory,
waiting for the event
to start, in which
I was to play
an integral part—

so integral, in fact,
that I was called in
in the afternoon
for a sound check
and run-through, to get
not only the sequence
in sync but the intricate
positioning and movement
of equipment and instruments
just so, for the full
theatrical effect—
which is why I was
sitting on the steps alone,
eyes closed, focusing,
going over things again,
and when I opened them,
the first star
beckoned in the autumn sky,
and I was about to make
a fitting wish
when, out of the corner
of my eye, I spotted
someone strolling over
from the grocery parking lot
who turned out to be
an acquaintance, a clerk
on break who naturally
asked what I was doing
there in the dark:
"Loitering," I said.
"People just don't
loiter like they used to.
We need to loiter more."
We laughed. And then
I told him the simple

truth about the event,
which he said he wished
he could attend,
and then to complicate
matters, I revealed
my near-wish on the star,
which he said was really
Jupiter and then left
to go back to work,
leaving me with the impression
of my own ignorance,
and how, in another
time and place,
or in this same place
but in another time,
we would have met
by designation to rehearse,
not so much a performance
but a different
kind of activity
staged in a clearing
and consisting
mostly of silence
and the entire community
listening to the creek
over there, the fire
crackling, and when
the right dark,
the right light
appeared in place, just so,
we would position our
selves in place, just so,
holding and raising
the products of harvest,
raising our faces

to that exact light
at the precise moment
just so the prescribed event
could happen, and we could
whisper, in unison,
not anything as remote
as "Jupiter"
but the name of our own
meaning and making
designated to express,
not so much
the products of knowledge
but a collective
feeling of fall and all
of the above
as we huddled in a forest
clearing surrounded
by sound, surrounded
by dark, surrounded
by the coming of winter,
watching sparks rise
in the direction
of that Great Light
known as "Retipuj."

Back *over here*
by the back door
is where my father
suffered a stroke
somewhere in the back
of his brain, bringing

birds in a gully
to the fore,
the scent of rain

hovering on horizons,
moss-covered rocks
gracing a shaded shore,

and a voice saying:
"Here, son—take
these. I won't be
needing them anymore."

And then,
for sure,
the camps
is where

over there
and
over here

converged.

Or, really, now—
when, and where,
does *over here*
become *over there?*

Over and under
Here and *there,*

In any fashion,
Is to be found

The very center
Of compassion.

II

the real inada

THE REAL INADA

If I had to choose one person of my greater clan to include in some listing of remarkable Americans, it would have to be my uncle Yoshitaro Inada. I was thinking about him the other day when I drove the old river road through the Sacramento delta, where my cousin Lily lives with her family on a farm below the levee. Many of our people settled there at the turn of the century, creating tiny, still-existing villages and orchards and farms. Although my uncle never lived there, I'm sure he approved and was proud of his daughter's choice of a husband.

He was that kind of guy—proud, supportive, traditional, and a man of the land. And his history was such that he could remain that way, maintain that way—relying on the integrity of his mind, his knowledge, his wits, his senses, and calling upon the resources of his body and community. As the saying goes, they don't make them like that anymore.

Yoshitaro, Uncle Y, was born in a southern Japanese village in 1890. Times were tough, life was hard; thus, his father left for America in 1896, followed by his mother in 1901, and it took them years of laboring on a Hawaii plantation to earn passage to California in 1905.

In the meantime, Yoshitaro and his sister (who eventually made her way to Brazil) were entrusted to the village for raising (Yoshitaro's grandfather, my great-grandfather, was a highly respected village healer and spiritual leader, who happened to be blind); thus, when Yoshitaro was finally sent for, in 1910, he was a fully formed individual. (My father was born that same year, on the Pajaro River in Watsonville.)

Which is to say that, unlike my father, who went on to become a dentist, Uncle Y never had to become "Americanized"—he never had to attend American schools, and he only had to learn enough English to get by (I would guess he acquired a driver's license, but perhaps not; I would also guess he knew some Spanish); in other words, Uncle Y could stay himself, which was considerable. This is not to say that an American education is not valuable, but what it often consists of, and how it is imparted, can have a negating effect on some; nor do I mean to imply that Yoshitaro was not an American; on the contrary, he was *very* American—an exemplary American, an embodiment of American ideals—but he just didn't speak much English.

He was about as American as, say, a Navajo. (And with his dark, handsome features, it is easy to picture him at home among their nation.) He considered this his home, even homeland, never wanting to return to Japan, and during World War II he sent his only son off to join the u.s. military, to serve with honor. But what truly exemplified his "American-ness" was his love of the *land*—the land itself (whatever it was labeled) and all that came with it—and this sense ran deeper than labels or lip service.

Because he truly loved and knew and appreciated the land—which included the creatures and vegetation. He lived with the land, on the land, and was *of* the land; he knew it as he knew his hands, and they went together, like harvest and rain, like sunsets and song.

Now by the time I came along and got to know the man, we were in a concentration camp in Arkansas, hard by the Mississippi. Uncle Y, not being one to take such things lightly, had brought a bunch of seeds with him and, in short order, with handmade implements, started not just a garden but a small farm. The camp was a standard, makeshift installation of fenced barracks and scraped ground, good for dust and mud; but that's not the way he saw it. And since he served on the work crew that went out into the swamp each day to chop firewood, he was able to smuggle in his various found-treasures: plants, more plants, some wild creatures, and special chunks of wood.

Burls too good to be burned. Burls with swirling grains and curved, angular shapes suitable for polishing and displaying, either as is or with tiny plants planted in orifices, becoming miniature landscapes, and one served to display his son's cards and letters from throughout Europe. So with handmade scrap-lumber furnishings to augment government cots, he and my aunt were rather comfortable, especially since, for the first time, they had indoor plumbing and running water—albeit a block away in the public laundry and communal toilet.

The one thing lacking, however, was a furo, a Japanese bath; thus, since Uncle Y had never taken a shower in his life and wasn't about to start, he quickly fashioned a furo out of, once again, scraps and ingenuity—and there it was, in the corner of the open shower stalls. It included a wooden-slatted area for soaping and rinsing, with a wooden bucket (handmade, I'm sure, along with the wooden stool). And the tub, of course, heated by a fire beneath, was strictly for soaking, steaming, sighing, singing—and the warm scent of wet wood served to negate the smell of industrial disinfectant. Eventually, Uncle Y might have invited his fellow laborers on the outside to come in and partake, to ease their aches from plantation cottonfields.

And while the rest of the camp proceeded in the prescribed, concentration-camp manner—grim, grimy, like a grainy black-and-white newsreel—my uncle transformed his barrack-grounds into a technicolor nature documentary. Everything from outside had made its way into the barrens to flourish, including fish and frogs and crawdads in the pond; the effect was not artsy either, but more like an extension of the swamp; as a result, many birds and insects gathered in the foliage, perhaps causing neighbors to complain of the noise (prisoners are supposed to be quiet); it was even rumored that, somewhere, ol' Yoshitaro kept a pet water moccasin.

Ah, yes, he could have stayed there forever, loving the land, being creative, productive, useful, extending himself to the greater community, but, alas, we were re-moved to a camp in the Colorado desert, where the land wasn't as fecund, but he managed to make do with a grand rock garden of cacti and sage, sandy, craggy home of scorpions, tarantulas, lizards, snakes, one old tortoise, and many birds. Then came recruiters for farm workers to combat the labor shortage, and Uncle Y was gone in a flash.

And didn't return. For he had managed to work his way clear up to northern Colorado, to an apparently beautiful place not far from Denver—a sugar beet farm on the high plains with the big sky and the grand landscape, looking out on the Rockies. "Rockies," he could say that all right. He had arranged for his wife to come and cook, on the same "work-release program," and even his elderly father, born in the 1860s, would serve as some sort of caretaker. The way they figured it, the bunkhouse beat the barracks—for the duration.

And then some. Because although the war went and ended, and we all reimmigrated to California, Yoshitaro and family stayed in Colorado! They enjoyed the sugar beet life, loved the grainy soil, the clear water, and, like the old days, had acquired some horses. And they'd write poetic letters praising the wonderfully extravagant thunderstorms, the luxurious snow, and the sparkling, gem-like hail.

Finally, however, in July 1947, after repeated requests, they consented to return to somewhat humdrum California and resume farming in the Santa Clara valley. Starting from scratch never bothered him; that entire region bore his "scratch marks," where he had helped build houses, roads, creating farms and sharecropping communities where there weren't any. It was his territory; time after time, remote, hidden places in the rocky, forbidding foothills had sprung forth with production, each furrow shaped into a Y.

34

After the war, though, he rented various preexisting farms, near Gilroy, and settled down as a respected elder of the community. He had certain admirable qualities that are talked about to this day: he knew everything there was to know about farming, of course, including weather patterns, which he could feel in his bones; he could repair any kind of machinery, including his vintage utility vehicle, a Crosley; he could be trusted to work—and work without complaining. Times had always been tough, but so was he; he was a man's man, a devoted father and son, and as a brother he supported my father through college. He never had much, but he had a lot.

And one thing he possessed was not his to own: respect. This was conferred by the community; thus, he was called upon to attend and participate in many significant events—weddings, funerals, anniversaries—in our greater San Jose region community because, well, just because he was a cultured, distinguished, sophisticated gentleman of presence, one to be entrusted with responsibility.

He could drink with the best, and tell the best jokes; he could give the best toasts—toasts that spoke like prophecy, for the whole community. And best of all, he could sing like no one else. And his singing, naturally, was not conventionally "American"; rather, it was older, and ran deeper, than the very concept of the nation itself. Some of the lyrics, for instance, contained ancient terms no longer in everyday usage; and his singing style demonstrated such mastery, range, and nuance that it was not to be taught, and certainly not learned, in conventional courses.

It had to be lived; and he had to partake of it, from infancy on, from his blind grandfather, at that old healer's knee. And in Uncle Y's singing, I could envision my great-grandfather, could hear the old one's voice saying, "Yoshitaro, Yoshitaro . . ." And the child would sing, displaying his comprehension of each word, each historical or mythological reference, and

35

the breathing would have to be just so, each pause in place. And for any blessing or healing to occur, the intonation had to be perfect, each rise, each fall, each guttural quaver emanating not so much from the throat and mouth but from the pit of the stomach, the bottom of the heart.

To my young ears, it all sounded rather strange, mysterious, but it was effective enough to silence us children without our being asked, to stop us in our tracks no matter what we were doing. We'd peer out from under banquet tablecloths to watch, and listen; and we'd look around the room at familiar faces and see glazed, unfamiliar expressions, eyes staring off into space as Yoshitaro sang, slowly intoning each syllable with such power and passion.

And when he was finished, the atmosphere was different—we could hear better, clearer, we would feel calmer, more at peace. And I imagine that, for the elders, it took quite some time to return from their journeys, and late that night, falling asleep, they'd still be departing misty villages, embarking on ships, arriving in challenging lands, laboring to raise families, and then those families, entire communities, would be embarking on trucks and trains to camp, eventually returning to this room in San Jose, where even the kitchen staff would be transfixed, lost in their journeys, at the kitchen door. And all I could do was whisper to another child: *"That's my Uncle Y."*

He wasn't a happy man; he was *contented*. And in his final years, he and family members finally managed to buy a farm, which they mostly tended to, enabling Yoshitaro to embark on his major project, the transformation of his *own American land*.

Surely, a vision came to him, looking out the kitchen window, seeing all that space, and the space was his. There was that old tree over there, and that other old tree over there, close enough for their branches to touch, but with enough space in between to set a barrack. He had to chuckle about that, smile his famous smile—and then he set immediately to work.

And since his was a world of cisterns and shovels, of bent nails sorted and stored in old fruit jars, and since he never knowingly wasted anything, he had all he needed to accomplish his vision. And what he created was Japan. California. Arkansas. Colorado. Plus.

Whatever grew anywhere, it was there. Whatever was not supposed to grow there, it was there. Tropics, desert, tundra—it was there. Things that needed delicate treatment, they were there, flourishing in his personal atmosphere. And when the public got word of what he was doing, friends and strangers alike would drop off plants in his care—rejects, diseased, whatever . . .

Even my wife, a certified "master gardener," would bring him sick exotic plants she had given up on, little spotted, droopy things on their last legs—and when we'd come by several months later, she couldn't recognize them! They probably didn't recognize themselves—because these little decorative houseplants would be well on their way to becoming big bushes, even trees! And there was this one tiny cactus that, even using an eyedropper just once a week, she had somehow overwatered, causing it to curl up and melt down to nothing. Well, when she saw it again, she thought Yoshitaro was lying or had replaced it with another, because he claimed he had talked to it, hosed it off a lot, and there it stood—like a blooming child! And it wasn't supposed to bloom until the 21st century . . .

He had so many plants that they created their own climate. Some were in the ground, others were at various levels, in tiers. Among the many bonsai trees were some that were not supposed to be—for instance, who ever heard of a miniature sequoia? But there it was, next to the tiny redwood, thriving on lyrics and mist . . .

So, as with the rest of the community, we had to take him

at his word—for he was known as a man of his word—and if he said he was doing some talking, we figured he was doing some tall talking. And listening. Because that's exactly what he did with the fish and frogs in the pond, the lizards on the moss, and all the birds in the foliage: talked and listened. But he didn't necessarily feed those creatures to alter or tame their nature; rather, they fed themselves in his organic environment. And although he built the pond and received the fish from friends, and although he built and hung some miniature barracks for the birds, the birds and other creatures relocated there on their own.

And every morning, he'd call them, and they'd come—some birds even perching on his shoulders. And several of these creatures had come to him for healing—desperate, wounded birds, maimed dogs, stray cats with broken legs; there was even a healed raccoon under the barn . . . then Uncle Y would be off among the plants, humming, talking, listening, singing . . .

He was just one man, one Inada in this country, and what he left behind wasn't much. And what could have become his legacy is pretty much decimated now, but not by choice: what the family realized, as soon as he died, was that it would take a whole crew of professional caretakers to maintain his space, to take his place, because each tree, each plant, had to be nurtured in an individual manner—and rather than have everything die, the family called upon the community to help assume the responsibility. So the people came, and came, and came, carting off some specimens that could be worth good money on the market.

So Yoshitaro's remarkable legacy lives on, endures in his home community. And as his nephew, I aspire to carry on his legacy of song, through my efforts in poetry—but I'm an ignorant upstart compared to him. And in the meantime, I sometimes stand outside and call the birds.

And sometimes they come.

DENVER UNION STATION

The crescent moon. Reminding me of that special
crescent rising like a crescendo over Colorado
as we made our way by special train
from Amache Camp to Denver,

where we would transfer
to all those special places we knew as home . . .

It was a slow train, some
Midnight Special, stacked and packed
with what was left of Amache;

it was a slow train, faster
than fences, faster than Amache
back there, back there, back there—
Amache, Amache, Amache, trying to catch us;

it was a slow train,
it was a slow moon,
as we rolled our way,
as we stole our way,
crossing Colorado . . .

Daybreak. The crack
of dawn, and a man in uniform
came stumbling down the aisle—
pushing, shoving, stepping over bodies,
shouting "Denver Union Station"
over and over: "Denver Union Station—
                    Everybody off!"—

and we were off, we *were*
off, off and running, scrambling
to seek connections to what we knew as home . . .

What to say of that journey?
Let's just say it was special;
let's just say it was eventful;
let's just say that special and eventful journey
continued long after we arrived in Fresno,
continued as it does to this very day,
to *every* day I wake up
not in Amache, *not* in Amache;

and as a matter of fact, you might say
we never left that station either,
because for years after,

my grandfather would call me into his living room,
would call me into his living room
to stand there, stationed, before his chair,

and the old man would put down his paper,
and the old man would whisper to his young grandson:

 "Rhosohn—do Denvah. Do Denvah."—

and the young grandson would stand there, stationed,
and the young grandson would intone, over and over,
chanting:

 "Denver Union Station!
 Denver Union Station!
 Denver Union Station!—
 Everybody off!"

40

And then there would be silence.
And there in the empty, echoing station
("Denver Union Station—Everybody off!")
the old man would look at the child,
their eyes would meet,
and they both would smile—

and the smile would be
("Denver Union Station!")
the smile of the journey,
their journey,

and the smile would be
("Denver Union Station!")
the smile, their smile,
and everybody's smile,

of freedom.

THE GRAND SILOS OF THE SACRAMENTO

From a distance, at night, they seem to be
industries—all lit up but not on the map;
or, in this scientific age, they could be
installations for launching rocket ships—
so solid, and with such security, are they . . .
Ah, but up close, by the light of day,
we see, not "pads" but actual paddies—
for these are simply silos in ricefields,
structures to hold the harvested grain.
Still, they're the tallest things around,
and, by night or day, you'd have to say
they're ample for what they do: storage.
And, if you amble around from your car,
you can lean up against one in the sun,
feeling warmth on your cheek as you spread
out your arms, holding on to the whole world
around you, to the shores of other lands
where the laborers launched their lives
to arrive and plant and harvest this grain
of history—as you hold and look, look
up, up, up, and whisper: *"Grandfather!"*

GRANDMOTHER

for Grandmothers Miju Inada and Yoshiko Saito

Except for the fact that Grandmother taught me
chopsticks and Japanese before forks and English,
my relationship with Her wasn't all that much.

As a matter of fact, Grandmother, with Her old-
fashioned ways, was actually somewhat of an extra-
vagant source of confusion and distraction.

For example, just to waste time on a rainy day
in a boring barrack room in our ordinary
concentration camp in Arkansas, She'd say:

"The Great God Thunder is very powerful.
Listen to Him. When He storms, be careful.
Or He will send Lightning to take your navel!"

Or, on just another quiet night in Colorado,
on the way to the shower house, She may pause
in the warm desert sand to simply say:

"Ah, the Full Moon! Look closely, Grandson.
It's the same Moon, and the same Story.
'Two Rabbits with Mallets Pounding Rice.'"

Time passes. Grandmother passes. I've learned
the facts since. Still, in some storms I feel
a twitch, and in the still of certain nights,

with the right chopsticks, I can eat with
the Rabbits who have scattered all the Rice.

Eatin' with Sticks

When you think about it,
eatin' with sticks
is the natural thing to do;

that is, without getting all
sociological about it,
it makes logical sense

to handle your food
with these smooth extensions
of your fleshy fingers—

that way, the hot
is truly cool,
bit by bit making its way

south to your mouth
as you choose
what you chews,

chowing down on, say,
succulent shoots of bamboo
with sticks of bamboo

as you come full circle
in the ecological
sense of things,

which makes good sense
and shouldn't
bamboozle any bambino

44

with a lick of sense,
a lick of taste,
and elders demonstrating

the social, logical value
of a world not to waste,
slash, stab at random,

not to just scoop around
like so many grains
of surplus and plenty.

Moreover, sticks
are never alone—
as in "sticks together,"

they are paired
like the very stereo
parts of the body—

arms, hands, legs, feet,
ears, eyes, molars,
nostrils of the nose,

with all of those
working together ricely,
in sync, as we eat . . .

But wait—what's missing?
Right—a whole person
does not a society make . . .

Thus, as any unshaven sage
in a mountain hermitage
will instruct you,

"You need a *bowl,* baby!"
Which is to say,
"You can't go it alone!"

And even a hermit
wouldn't be here
if it weren't for

sticks *and* bowls,
the whole enchilada
of Yin and Yang,

of boys and girls,
of what makes the world
worth sitting down with,

wherever you are,
blessing the bowl
of food, community,

collective memory,
creative heritage,
the grains, the noodles

that wouldn't have it
any other way:
"Eat us with STICKS!"

In a Buddhist Forest

Even if you're not Buddhist,
Even if you don't know
Anything about Buddhism,

Even if you're not interested
In its precepts and paths,
Even if you're anti-Buddhist,

Your Buddhist Self proceeds
Accordingly, in a Buddhist city,
In a Buddhist forest . . .

KICKING THE HABIT

Late last night, I decided to
stop using English.
I had been using it all day—

    talking all day,
    listening all day,
    thinking all day,
    reading all day,
    remembering all day,
    feeling all day,

    and even driving all day,
    in English—

when finally I decided to
stop.

So I pulled off the main highway
onto a dark country road
and kept on going and going
until I emerged in another nation and . . .
stopped.

There, the insects
inspected my passport, the frogs
investigated my baggage, and the trees
pointed out lights in the sky,
saying,
    "Shhhhlllyyymmm"—

and I, of course, replied.
After all, I was a foreigner,
and had to comply . . .

Now don't get me wrong:
There's nothing "wrong"
with English,

and I'm not complaining
about the language
which is my native tongue.
I make my living with the lingo;
I was even in England once.
So you might say I'm actually
addicted to it;
yes, I'm an Angloholic,
and I can't get along without the stuff:
It controls my life.

Until last night, that is.
Yes, I had had it
with the habit.

I was exhausted,
burned out,
by the habit.
And I decided to
kick the habit,
cold turkey,
right then and there
on the spot!

And, in so doing, I kicked
open the door of a cage
and stepped out from confinement
into the greater world.

Tentatively, I uttered,

    "Chemawa?   Chinook?"

and the pines said

    "Clackamas, Siskiyou."

And before long, everything else
chimed in with their two cents' worth
and we had a fluid and fluent
conversation going,

    communicating, expressing,
    echoing whatever we needed to
    know, know, know . . .

What was it like?
Well, just listen:

Ah, the exquisite seasonings
of syllables, the consummate consonants, the vigorous
vowels of varied vocabularies

    clicking, ticking, humming,
    growling, throbbing, strumming—

coming from all parts of orifices, surfaces,
in creative combinations, orchestrations,
resonating in rhythm with the atmosphere!

I could have remained there
forever—as I did, and will.
And when I resumed my way,
my stay could no longer be

    "ordinary"—

as they say,
as *we* say, in English.

For on the road of life,
in the code of life,

there's much more to red than

     "stop,"

there's much more to green than

     "go,"

and there's much, much more to yellow than

     "caution,"

for as the yellow
sun clearly enunciated to me this morning:

     "Fusao. Inada."

III

ringing the bell

Ringing the Bell

I. THE MAN OF LETTERS

Picture this: A man of letters is sitting on a curb in a quiet, shady neighborhood. He has decided to visit his childhood home and is basking in the warmth, reflecting on the past and the path that life has taken him.

Ah, yes—it had been quite a journey . . . after all these years, decades even . . . and now, had he so chosen, he could have filled his car to overflowing with his innumerable publications, and there would still have been enough books remaining to create a high seat on the curb.

Ah, yes—it had been quite a journey . . . who would have thought? . . . He can practically hear the locomotive clanging on that misty morning when he left to seek his way in the world . . .

II. THE MAN OF ICES

As it turned out, that dreamy sound was a real bell, tinkling around the corner. And then there appeared, in broad daylight, a tiny old Mexican man slowly pushing a wobbly, makeshift cart. And then the neighborhood, my neighborhood, suddenly came to life, with doors opening, elders of varying ancestry—African, Asian, Latin American, American Indian—standing on porches, and children with coins rushing to greet the man.

And as the bell stopped, their melodious voices began— ah, such choices of colors and flavors, the multitude of Mexican ices rising from the mist of his mysterious contraption. I stood there, simply another customer for *una fresa,* strawberry, but there passed between us a glint of recognition, because, old as he was, old as I was, he was the same old man serving the same old child, smiling . . .

The old man, *el viejo,* quite obviously, is a significant part of our community. He is not just a vendor—not by any means—but a highly respected and appreciated elder, one who engenders trust and a sense of mutuality, one whose very presence is an embodiment of values. His presence is, as the saying goes, clear as a bell.

And you might say his was a bell of freedom for a child from the shadowy barrens of confinement, a bell summoning that child to dash freely into the sunny street to not only exchange currency for a delicacy of sweetness but to do so in a place where he belonged.

Belonged, belonged, belonged. In *mi tierra,* my homeland, my home.

IV. STRIKING THE WORDS

I've never left; I've brought it with me; it's who I am. And what I am is a product of my community—nothing more, nothing less. My father was born in back of a noodle factory; my mother was born in back of a fish store; those facts are at the forefront of my being. And I was born to a time, and in a place, in which great gifts were bestowed upon me. How privileged could I be? It was the *people* who made me, who granted me what I can only acknowledge, never repay. And in my own modest way, I attempt to strike the right words, the right words, to convey what there is to say . . .

V. "LA BAMBA"

After the war, we lived for a while in my grandparents' home (the home and family fish store had been entrusted to longtime friends) while my father picked peaches and grapes, eventually saving enough to resume his dental practice and rent a home several blocks away.

The very first day, I simply went across the street to play at the Palomino home, with their boys, Henry and Herb, only a few months separating us in age. And for the next decade or so, there were very few days when I *wasn't* at the Palomino home. They had five children, and I simply became the sixth; they even gave me my own name: Grandmother called me Losano, but little Sylvia said I was Chano, as I've been since.

Someone was always singing, so I learned Spanish through song. On summer days, we'd sit around in the shade of a fragrant orange tree, listening to the women in the backyard, in the open shelter called the "summer kitchen," humming as they made soap, made tortillas, worked with harvests from the garden—cactus, chiles, corn, squash, tomatoes, beans . . . and I could always stay to eat . . .

Sometimes we'd sleep out on the lawn, talking, envisioning, listening to the music of distant cantinas drifting through the trees: "Yo no soy marinero . . ." Ah, bells of morning, early mass . . .

It was a place of warmth, respect, tradition, and values, and we grew up that way. When we came of age, we went to work—toiling with grown men for 85 cents an hour in the wrinkling heat of a sprawling West Fresno fruit-drying yard. But it was good work, honest labor, and we became strong men who went on with our lives.

And, of course, the scents, the flavors, the sweat, the love, are still in the song to be sung: " . . . soy capitàn, soy capitàn . . ."

VI. "SWING LOW . . ."

When the Jones family moved in across the street from my grandparents, my academic interests expanded accordingly. In grade school, I simply listened to the music a lot, but in junior high, Sam Jones and I seriously began to study it, and his home became our conservatory.

What made Sam's home special was all the history it contained. Whereas all the local jukeboxes contained a full range of the current music, from gospel to bop, the Jones collection spanned decades. When I visited my grandparents, which was often, I also went to study at the Jones classroom.

The front room, where the big old phonograph was, and where much of the collection was stacked. All fragile 78s, of course, which the family had seen fit to carry from Georgia. Which spoke of priorities. The family also spoke in the traditional way, as in "carry"; and when the parents called you "child," it meant just that.

Now, since Reverend Jones was a minister, the music was "sacred" (albeit in a dazzling variety of musical styles), but Sam's older brother had his own collection of mostly jazz, and we would "steal" into his room and bring things out to play. We went on hearsay (Lester Young and Charlie Parker were household words), advice from Sam's brother, and our own ears—and before long we could recite "chapter and verse" regarding the music.

All the music, sacred and secular—spirituals, blues, rhythm and blues, jazz—all flowed together in one beautiful "Deep River," and even a humorous tune like Dizzy Gillespie's "Swing Low, Sweet Cadillac" could carry a child to church. Singing, swinging, shining!

Then, after a while, we'd go humming down to Tulare and G, where Reverend Jones was preaching on the corner. He would play the accordion, Mrs. Jones would play the guitar, and Sam's little sister would play the tambourine; they would all sing, and it would be more beautiful than anything on record . . .

VII. RINGING

Clear as a bell. Ringing, ringing, ringing, ringing . . .

The Real Fresno

for my beloved brother
Henry Palomino, 1938–1996

The way I figure it,
and sure live it,
Fresno, although
founded by the railroad

in a serious
valley venture
of exploitation,
steal, and ties,

is actually
a port town,
with dirt simply
being a slightly

different variety
of water.
Which is why
those of us

of the colored
sector down
by the docks
were versed in,

immersed in,
observant of,
devoted to,
fascinated by,

and continually
concerned with
the ebb and flow,
the fall and rise,

the known depths,
the shifting shallows,
and current
currents of jive!

Residue

If you were, oh,
this tasty shade of brown
or beyond, or had a light-
complected Spanish name,
"Frank H" is where you swam.

Not that you couldn't make
it to a river or a lake,
but as a kid you didn't;
and as for those deep,
steep irrigation ditches,
well, remember those friends . . .

So since summer hit hundreds
from May through September,
you tended to laze around
Frank H. Ball Playground
with that pool in the corner.

Small and inadequate, sure,
but, boy, it sure was cool!
Just show up with some coins
and you could not be refused.

Moreover, here, we had safety
in numbers, because not only
could you feel at home,
but with teeming multitudes
jostling in that water,
it was impossible to drown!

Wall-to-wall brown!
The Ganges of Chlorine!
And the friendly city
caste-system allowed you to
splash around for free
on designated cleaning days . . .

Lower, lower went the level.
Harder, harder scrubbed
brushes at the residue . . .

Come morning, their luminous
pool was all filled up—
ready to welcome the kids
not even chlorine could cut.

MESSING WITH THE SISTERS

No matter how bad you were,
or tried to be,
there was always some Sister
who had your number.

It might be in a physical way,
if you were fool enough
to fool with, oh,
     Johnnie Jewel Jennings
     or Big Lencha Martinez
     or Little Corrine Kim
     with her convincing kicks,
or any anonymous
girl on the playground
who all by her lonesome
had Sisters at home;

then, too, as we learned
early, later on,
any Sister had the capability
of putting some big hurt
on your heart—

so why in the world
would you mess with a Sister?

Because to mess with a Sister
was to mess with your Mother.

NOBODY, NOTHING

Big Lencha, just because
I was small
and standing there,
smiling,
as she lost
her turn at jacks,

chased me
all the way home
and stood there,
shaking her fist
at the window.

Huff-puff, huff-puff,
phew, as I
turned on the radio.

"Who's that out there?"
"Nobody, Mom."
"What's she doing?"
"Nothing."

Well, the program
ended, night fell,
dinner came
and went—

but there was Lencha.

Now, I kid you not
when I reveal
that, as things

were wont to happen
in youth and Fresno,

she stayed there
like a fixture
day and night
through several
seasons, long enough

to be taken
for granted
by the accepting
community . . .

But, as you
might guess,

the expected
happened at dusk,
on Labor Day—

Lencha simply
lowered her fist,
like some tired
Statue of Liberty,
shrugged, shook
off the stuff
and went home.

Except
I followed, stood
outside all night,
and that morning
tracked her
like a shadow
to school—

where, since it was
the first day,
I changed
my schedule
to sit beside
her in basic
home economics,
intermediate
sewing, introductory
stenography—

because, you see,
Big Lencha
had become
a different person,

a smaller, larger
version named Lorenza,
with mysterious
scents and tresses,

and a smiling answer
for her surly father
inquiring about
the unsmiling youth
sulking on the lawn:

"Nobody, nothing."

Hiroshi from Hiroshima

I. SMALL THINGS

He was "Hiroshi from Hiroshima."
That's all I knew about him.
Along with the fact that
he arrived early and stayed late.
And, for such a big, strong man,
we were all surprised
by how little he ate—

some small things
wrapped in a small paper bag,
a bag he folded carefully,
and brought back the next day.

This was the summer of 1954.
I was working in my grandfather's
famous fish store
and busy doing three things:

   1. Making payments on my new,
     metallic blue '49 Ford,
     which, for 1954
     and eight hundred bucks,
     was worth working for;

   2. Working out at night,
     running along country roads
     with friends, in anticipation
     of our senior football season;

   3. Trying to figure out a way
     to approach a certain person.

And, oh, there were some cool clothes
down the street at the Peacock Department Store.

II. PARALLEL LIVES

Hiroshi, I believe, had some connections
with my grandfather. Some network
was at work, some relations
in the way that all people from the old country
appeared to be part of one family.

And maybe they were.
For instance, it wasn't until long after
my grandfather had passed
that I found out, in passing,
that he had had another family in Japan,
that his first wife had died over there,
and somewhere over there
were his grandchildren my age,
and we were leading parallel lives.

III. SKILL

So, early one morning, Hiroshi arrived.
Or, rather, he was already there
when I arrived with my uncles to open the door.
They nodded at him (I had never seen him before),
and he immediately went to work.

Now, the strange (or interesting) thing is,
except for office or telephone work
(which I didn't know how to do, either;
but I could drive, picking up and delivering
all over greater Fresno, including
outback country towns),

well, Hiroshi could do everything.
From the minute he put on his apron,
he could do it all.
And with such efficiency, grace, and skill
that by the next day he was already
the favorite of our regular customers.

These old people would come in—
people of many colors, languages,
places of origin—

and wait for him to wait on them.

IV. WAITING FOR HIROSHI

Actually, it was "uncanny," as they say—
because here was this new guy,
just off some boat, in a new country,
and instead of being like a fish out of water,

he was functioning proficiently
by some kind of telepathy.
Looking back, I'd say there was some kind of
immigrant empathy involved, some kind of
mutuality at work, some kind of
unstated message communicated

which comes down to *trust,*
which comes down to *understanding*
what you've all gone through
back home, down home, and here,

as you stand, waiting for Hiroshi.

V. SAMURAI

So, yes, these elders would come in,
point, signal, nod, whatever,
and whatever it was they wanted,
they got: fresh, sparkling,
                        personalized to perfection.

Say they wanted a pound chunk
off that big piece of sea bass;
Hiroshi would size it up, slice
like a samurai, zap—one pound!

Say they wanted that whole chicken,
those squid, that abalone,
fixed just so—plus,
wrapped in ice for the trip back home;
they got it, precisely.

Say you needed something
for soup or stew,
or some friends were coming
over for barbecue
and you needed that rascal
skinned and filleted just so;
there it was, exactly.

And the next time, happy,
you'd come and tell Hiroshi,
in your smile and language,
just how great it was . . .

VI. UNPREFERRED

Maybe I didn't exactly feel rejected,
but I had to get used to being "unpreferred"—

by these elders, including relatives,
who always waited for Hiroshi.

But I didn't feel threatened—
because there were always

other things to do, others to wait on,
and, as both my uncles took vacations

and my grandfather came in less and less,
I was even given duties in the office;

thus, I made deliveries, answered the phone,
and urged Hiroshi that it was time to close.

VII. BETTER

One thing I learned that summer:
I was "pretty good," I was "okay,"
but I could learn to get better.

VIII. WAR

Not that I was going to take over the store.
My way lay across the tracks, at college.

And the way things were going in West Fresno,
with old businesses not meeting new codes,

and whole buildings being torn down
in the war called Urban Renewal,

something we didn't want to face
stared at us like a gap-toothed smile:

our home, this ethnic, colored district,
had seen its day, was giving way

to empty space; thus, the fish market
is now a parking lot where nobody parks.

IX. WATCH

So, that summer,
I learned
my place—

one of the
young ones,
one of the
new ones,

a good kid
at heart,
but without
the wherewithal
and wisdom
of decades
of survival.

You earn
respect.
You pay for
trust.
You experience
experience.

In the meantime,
here was a kid
you had to watch—

a kid who could
crush your tofu
while wrapping
with one hand

and waving at a
passing girl
with the other.

You had to watch
him while he weighed;
you had to supervise
at his shoulder
as he cut; otherwise,
you'd get home
and be surprised;

you had to watch
him on prices;
you had to watch
him on change.

Watch that kid!
Watch what's
going on
all around!

Next week, that kid
and everything else
will be gone!

X. HIROSHIMA

Still, perhaps some things never change.
Because another interesting, strange thing is
no one had to show Hiroshi the ropes—

because from that very first day,
he not only knew how we did things
(including making blocks of ice
in a buried tank of saltwater),

or where things were, he also knew
where we kept every little thing stored.

So this store, which my grandfather claimed
he designed and started from nothing
in 1912, as the first such store in the region,
just may have been part of something—

an ancient, time-honored, archetypal pattern
of workable history and proven tradition;

thus, Hiroshi, had he answered the phone,
might have said: "Hello, Hiroshima Fish Store!"

XI. MEZU-RAH-SHI

As it was, with my limited Japanese,
we only exchanged few words.

And usually it was "mezu-rah-shi!"—
his way of saying "How special!"

And I'd nod, acknowledging his quaint way
of acknowledging the very ordinary.

74

For instance, the very ordinary, daily,
early morning trip to the train depot

was usually cause for a "mezu-rah-shi"
or two; sometimes, just crossing the tracks

would do (well, looking back, I suppose
those tracks *were* special, since they seg-

regated people into colored and white);

he always said it while waiting for ordinary
freight or (dining) passenger trains to pass . . .

Then, at the depot, there'd be those
"mezu-rah-shi" crates to lift and load—

big as dripping coffins, slippery, hazardous
and heavy for our steel hooks to handle . . .

We'd grunt, shove, lift, shove some more,
and after I'd sign for the stuff, feeling

proprietary, the station clerk would offer us
ordinary coffee in ordinary paper cups . . .

XII. ACKNOWLEDGING THE QUALITIES

But that wasn't the half of it,
since back at the store
there was all that
relifting, unpacking, repacking to do,
which, in my fashion,
consisted of a lot of slamming,
bashing, breaking, crunching,
while Hiroshi calculatedly

undid his crates like packages,
salvaging each intact board,
each nail in a pile—

all the while
acknowledging the qualities
of human-sized halibut from Alaska,
salmon thick as thighs
from the Oregon coast,
big-eyed bottom-dwellers of the Baja,
and masses of slippery, prickly,
sometimes wriggling
shrimp or squid or perch
or mackerel or even octopi
from as far away
as the waters of Hawaii
and the Gulf of Mexico . . .

And everything, every single day,
while being repacked in fresh, clean ice,
merited a "mezu-rah-shi!"

XIII. GRAIN

Then there were the crates of jars
and canned goods from all over the world—

each item feeling special
on its way to the shelves.

And as for the sacks of rice, of course!
Tons of rice, stacks of rice

from Arkansas, Texas, California—
grain by mezu-rah-shi grain.

XIV. THE LITTLE DETAILS

Sometimes, he'd work alongside
my semiretired grandfather
for hours, placing pieces of salmon
to cure in miso casks. And the way

they carried on, talking, talking
about such common, ordinary things,

I got the impression that it didn't
take much to get grown men focused
on the little details of life . . .

And Hiroshi was not only a grown man,
but he may have had a wife . . .

XV. FIRST STRING

I, too, was a man,
and when the big semi
full of rice arrived,
I was more than ready
for those 100-pound sacks,

and it took deftness,
quickness, strength,
skill, and balance
to hoist and shoulder
each sack, careful
not to slip as you

made your wary way
from the street, through
the busy store, past
the walk-in refrigerator,

the walk-in freezer, to
the musty storage room.

One trip, and you
started to sweat;
two trips, and you
breathed real breath.

Hiroshi, however, seeing
all that, all that rice,
got into a mezu-rah-shi
trance, stuck a sack
under each thick arm
like taking toddler
twins off to bed,
and had the truck
unloaded in no time,
before the surprised
driver finished a Coke.

Another thing I learned
that summer: I may
have been first string
in football, but, boy,
this man was a *rope!*

XVI. MOHT-TAI-NAI

Then there was that other word:
    "Moht-tai-nai"—

    "What a shame"
        and
    "What a waste"
        combined.

Hiroshi first uttered this
over an open crate of clams—
live clams, but some whose
shells had broken in transit.

We had to throw those away.
"Moht-tai-nai, moht-tai-nai."

All day.

XVII. FOUNDING CONCEPTS

When I think about it,
those two words—
mezu-rah-shi and

moht-tai-nai—were
the founding concepts
of the very business:

my grandfather's genius
was knowing his special
customers and special fish;

thus, everything was fresh,
and very little was wasted.
Plus, grandfather and fish
were honest—take his word
and their flesh for it:
"Fresh" means fresh!

The only time my grandfather
made a mistake in ordering
was when he called the same

old fishery in San Diego
on a busy December day:

"We don't sell fish to Japs!"

XVIII. COMBINED

Oh, well—he had heard worse
since 1907, when he had arrived.
He was ready, and still fresh.
Thus, the concentration camps
were just mezu-rah-shi and
moht-tai-nai combined.

XIX. IN WHATEVER LANGUAGE

I think about that all the time.
Not a day goes by when someone
doesn't reflect upon those words—
mezu-rah-shi and *moht-tai-nai*—
in whatever language, as the two
words that best depict the history,
landscape, and people of America.

XX. BLESSINGS AND CONNECTIONS

At the end of that summer,
before Hiroshi left (wherever
he went, I'm sure it was with
my grandfather's blessings and connections),
and before I got my set of new, tubeless,
whitewall tires, along with full-moon hubcaps,
we had to make our seasonal
excursion to the dump.

Now, the advantages of living in West Fresno
were several:
    1. Boy, it sure was multicultural—
      or we were at least as colorful
      as those splendid species of fish;

    2. Gee, we sure had e-z access
      to the new Highway 99 freeway—
      which cut a huge swath through
      the middle of our side of town,
      displacing families, churches,
      businesses, whole neighborhoods
      in the process, concretely cut-
      ting our community in half and
      stranding my grandfather's home
      on the bank of a traffic-river;

    3. Gosh, we sure had fun playing
      Monopoly in institutional,
      "colored-coded" housing projects

      (as they did in making camps,
      somebody else always made good
      money in community development);

    4. Wow, despite our fabled, exotic
      "China Alley" and our authentic,
      ethnic, historic business district
      in the fabled heart of California,
      we didn't have to hassle tourists
      experiencing the real experience;

    5. And, right-o—we had the city dump!

So I took the truck around to the back of the store,
in the alley, where we stored the trash

(and where, in the old days, in the American
back-of-business tradition, my mother was born);

now, instead of a tiny house and yard,
only an ancient, fragrant orange tree remained—
the rest was space for delivery vans to back into,
and over in the corner was the trash.
Rather, it used to be a pile of trash—
smashed planks and crumpled cardboard—
but Hiroshi had managed to dismantle
and reassemble everything into symmetrical
stacks according to size, so that it resembled
a lumberyard and recycling center combined;

thus, the trash took on a kind of value—
which is why, several times, I surprised
fleeing winos making off with our trash!

(And come to think of it, my grandfather
built a dandy doghouse and little storage shed
with those fish-crate boards, so I suppose
those winos built a structure for sleeping.)

Whatever, it was still trash bound for the dump.
Hiroshi loaded up the truck in nothing flat
while I chatted with an old high school friend
and new streetwalker at the end of the alley.

We were ready for our trip to the dump!
Along the way, I remembered how exciting
it had been for me, a kid out of the camps,
to go with my dad in our rackety Model A
hauling our actual backyard's extravagant
surplus of, hard to believe, branches and leaves,
and along the way the kid might get a Pepsi.

One time, without telling anyone, I walked
out there with Gilbert Martinez, exploring,
and we came back riding on a bike he found.

And later on, we'd ride out there on bicycles,
and we always found something—and once,
on the same day, Gilbert found a puppy and a gun.

So, yes, a trip to the dump was something.
It was like an adventurous journey to the mountains,
because those massive, smoldering mounds
were like volcanoes, the tallest things around,
and it was dangerous out there, and to get there
you went through several geographical changes.

First, you went through your shady neighborhoods;
then, you passed the wasteland of projects;
then, when you got to the outskirts of town,
you were "down South" in the cottonfields,

where, way out there by the monstrous slaughterhouse,
beyond the massive, choking, smoking tallow works,
way out there beyond the Snake Road Hut, surrounded
by cottonfields, was the roadhouse known as Jericho.

Jericho, it was rumored, had a sentinel on the roof
who could spot plainclothes cops coming for miles.
Jericho, we knew very well, had some sentinel dogs
that, if they weren't chained, would have you
and your bicycle (and maybe your car) for supper.

So I was tooling along, hummin', reminiscin',
making sure the load was steady,
not paying much mind to Hiroshi,
who was a quiet guy anyway,

and when we arrived at the dump,
I'm the one who said "mezu-rah-shi,"

figuring the size and scope of the place
would impress him—

but nope, he didn't say a thing.

And then, after I back up to unload—
backing up to one of the many mounds,
finding a smooth way through the rubble,
watching out for glass,
watching out for metal,
watching out for wood with nails—

this is when, for the first and only time,
Hiroshi decides to get lazy.

That is, I'm up on the truck, with gloves,
grunting and shoving and tossing
things off like crazy,

while Hiroshi, with bare fingers, carefully
picks and chooses
pieces of wood,
pieces of cardboard,
and goes over there, slowly, seriously,
to lay them in neat and separate piles.

And then, while I'm working up a decent sweat,
he proceeds to stop altogether.
And just stands there!

And here's this big, strong guy,
this grown man,

84

just standing there with his hands at his sides,
looking around at the smoldering piles,
shaking his head
and gazing about
with this glazed look in his eyes,
muttering:
    "Moht-tai nai!
    Moht-tai-nai!
    Moht-tai-nai!
    Moht-tai nai!"

A Nice Place

Outside the rest home,
resting in his
wheelchair in the shade,

my father said:
"This is a nice place."

And I couldn't tell
if he meant

    the rest home
    in general,
    the shady space
    with the birds
    chirping, fountain
    flowing, spring
    breezes blowing,

or the world.

IV

putting back the rain

Putting Back the Rain

Because it was raining,
and I wanted to be
dry and outside,
I decided to
put back the rain
from where it came,

and went about the yard
gathering raindrops,
one by one by one,
and throwing them,
one by one by one,
back up into the air

where they stuck,
one by one by one,
above my head,
and before I knew it
I had a fine rain-roof,

a roof of rain
that was shining
like a stream
and wouldn't let
the wet rain through.

Pursuing a Career

I. WRITING

Writing in cursive,
long-
hand,
it occurs to me

how those long-
handed people
cursed aboard
penmanship

and sailed away.

II. WORD PROCESSING

Intern(m)e(n)t.

III. MY LICENSE

Way, way back, when I was still
considering careers,
the factory foreman told me
he was attending night school
because "being a plumber
      in New York City
      is like having
      a license to print money."

I'm sure Lenny's doing just that now,
whereas here I am in the boonies,
plumbing the depths for minimal currency

with my license to print poetry.

IV. SHOULDERING RESPONSIBILITY

When the sales of my new book
went zooming over the two-thousand mark,
I immediately whipped over
to the neighboring town of Phoenix, Oregon,
just to get a feel
of what the impact of my work might be.

Hard to imagine, but it's like every person—
man, woman, child—
in this equivalent community
possessed a copy of my book.

Imagine that!—like I could cruise
into Karla's Kut 'n' Kurlette
and get conversant about verses;
like I could drive thru Duane's Kwik Lube
spoutin' haiku all the while;
like I could bop about Uncle Bob's
Video and Comic Shoppe
to find my stuff under Action and Adult.

Shouldering such responsibility,
I was actually relieved
when the kid behind the MiniMart counter
kept sipping his Big Gulp

and did *not* let on I was me.

V. FAX

Grandparents,
as you ready to
leave the homeland,

please attempt to
understand that,
thanks to your efforts,

your grandson
will eventually
rent a sleek

Japanese vehicle
in Grand
Rapids, Michigan.

VI. PAX

It's about time
you visited me
last night, as
drifting flakes.

VII. THANKS

Thank you
for joining me
in Karaoke
Poetry.

A WORLD OF PASSENGERS

The Bosnians are having breakfast
in the next booth.
Middle-aged flannel, working-class caps,
ordering off the menu
without any trouble.

The young Croatian couple
perch at the counter—
dressed for church, in a moderate hurry.
She's tiny as a grandmother
or a girl, with high-swirled hair,
little black shoes swinging in the air.

Meanwhile, two Armenians
occupy a corner in the sunny space
reserved for parties of four or more.
But they're old, formally dressed.
That commands respect.
Besides, the man needs a place
to place his hat, and the woman
does have a very large purse.

A family with children—
of as-yet-undetermined extraction—
embarks from a car
in the sparkling parking lot.

Now the southbound bus arrives,
permitting a world of passengers
to yawn, stretch, and dine
in this yawning stretch of countryside . . .

See you next time.

A High-Five for I-5

*

Archaeologists have determined
that the I-5 Corridor
was originally a Power Path
with sacred Prayer Places
accessible on the side.

*

Padre Yo-Cinco
headed forth
with a mission:

Each settlement now
has its own
Taco Bell.

*

The Chinese
are still blasting
I-5 into Canada.

*

I-5 is still being
excavated in Mexico.

*

I-5 is the only structure
to have its traffic
reported from the moon.

94

*

At any given moment,
there is enough water
in I-5 plastic bottles
to dampen a famine.

*

At any given moment,
there are more boats
on I-5 than off Cuba.

*

At any given moment,
there is more lifestyle
on I-5 in Seattle
than there ever was in Russia.

*

At any given moment,
there are more Asians
on I-5 than others
may care to imagine.

*

At any given moment,
there are more random
acts of kindness on I-5
than in medieval times.

*

If you were to chop up I-5
and lay it side by side,
you could easily cover Europe,

not to speak of encountering
unspeakable resentment.

*

If you were to roll up I-5
you could truthfully promote
the world's largest replica
of a butterfly tongue.

*

The combined cracks of I-5
are equal to the Grand Canyon.

*

The depth of I-5
is to be respected.

*

There are more I-5 reflectors
than stars in the galaxy.

*

I-5 paint can
readily cover
rain forests.

*

I-5 dashboards emit
more radiation than
all wars combined.

*

Residents east of I-5,
to the Atlantic Ocean,
are noticeably different
from those on the other side.

*

Within a 24-hour period,
I-5 roadkill could sustain,
for life, Santa's entourage.

*

The I-5 Litter Patrol
has no chance of parole.

*

All I-5 homeless
are licensed.

*

All I-5 music
is approved.

*

With the advent
of drive-thru schooling,
the Ramp Generation
never has to leave I-5.

*

The I-5 CEO's RV
is refueled while moving.

*

A proven fact:
I-5 drivers
via mirrors
read faster
backwards.

*

If ratified,
I-5 becomes
the world's
narrowest
nation.

*

Otherwise, I-5
remains the most-
traveled Möbius strip.

*

The I-5 median strip
is a designated reservation.

*

And, yes, the buffalo
have returned to I-5.

*

Improved sensors
allow many I-5 trucks,
especially at night,
to be driven by
the visually impaired.

*

98

In remote stretches,
beware of 1-5 hijackers
and false interchanges.

*

Coming soon:
The 1-5 Channel.

*

Being tested
in the Gulf:
The 1-5 Auto.

*

Almost extinct:
The 1-5 Bronco.

*

Always available:
The 1-5 Franchise.

*

Already in effect:
The 1-5 Interstate
Date Line.

Seeking the Great

I'm not sure I've ever seen,
or been seen by, or been seen with,
a great blue heron.

For instance, out of ignorance,
those big birds of recent rivers—
the Klamath and the Rogue—

or the rivers of my youth—
the Kings and the San Joaquin—
just might have been very average

sandhill cranes, although creating
somewhat sizeable
absorption as I stood there

unsoaring, stuck in the mud,
letting memory make myth
of the experience . . .

So what's so "great" about the GBH?
Oh, I suppose if one came up to you,
or spread its wings in a dream,

or just stood there fluorescently
at the foot of your bed,
you'd certainly know it;

or perhaps even a fledgling
flapping in your yard
might make its name known . . .

In the meantime, though, I'm grateful
to the great blue for allowing me
to consider the lesser fowl:

the okay jay atop a sunflower,
the regular robin on the lawn,
the generic sparrow in the bush—

all surrounding this common human
on this most ordinary Indian summer morning.

Picture

for Janet, Miles, and Lowell

Picture yourself in this painting.
Come in, please. Make yourself at home.
We'll do whatever we can
to make you feel at ease, welcome.

What brings you out this way?
You don't say. Please stay and visit.
And please don't mind appearances,
or what appears to be apprehension.

It is and it isn't. That is,
things are in the air, on the horizon,
but that's just the way it is,
has been, will be. And we'll all
settle in to a comfortable adjustment.

So how have you been? And the family?
Ah, so it goes. That's good to know.
And as a matter of fact, should you so
desire, or require, please feel free
to become one of us.

Yes. It doesn't take much to
picture yourself in this painting
as one of us, an archetypal family.

Which one are you?
Or who would you like to be?
Simply step in back of the painting
and enter from the other side.
Instead of a head, there's a hole.

And, since we're an obliging family,
feel free to make alterations accordingly
regarding gender, age, clothes . . .

Go ahead, strike any pose.
For this is your family now.
And this is your painting now.

Are we missing anyone? Include.
Are there too many of us? Dispose.
Would you prefer to be alone?
Do so. We're an obliging family.
Picture yourself as you will.

Actually, we're an obliging humanity.
We were there. We've seen it all.
We've been it all—conflict, loyalty . . .

And how you choose to portray yourself
significantly fits the picture . . .

So what else is new under the sun?
Picture *anyone* in this painting.
And once that's done, let's get down
to the business at hand—

shaking hands, smiling, embracing,
laughing in whatever language,
and just generally doing whatever it takes

to continue the journey we began in this painting.

TAPPING THE TEMPLES

Milton and I are
becoming old men—
old Jewish and Japanese men,
in the grand tradition.

And when we meet on the street,
in the course of conversation,
we always point to our heads,
tapping the temples

to indicate what's "upstairs,"
where the experience is,
where the knowledge is kept,
where the cash is counted out

coin by coin by coin,
where language is coined,
where the truth says,
"No work, no eat,"

where roots are treasures,
where youth is measured
by contribution to family,
where clothes are tailored

to fit each generation
that can't afford the luxury
of attending universities
as we did,

to lead the life
of men of letters

leading to retirement,
which is why

Milton and I always
point to our heads,
tapping the temples
where the dead

grandfathers live.

V

drawing the line

A Poet of the High Seas

I am a poet of the high seas,
My craft the craft of poetry,
Adaptable to all conditions
That await me on my journeys.

I am a poet of the high seas.
Such is my given calling.
The elders saw it in the stars
And guided me in my destiny.

I am a poet of the high seas.
I travel from land to land,
Through waves of water, sand,
Tides and currents of history.

I am a poet of the high seas.
I call on distant ports—
Familiar, forbidden, forgotten,
Crossroads of collective memory.

I am a poet of the high seas.
No storm can deny me.
My rhythms ride the wind
Through disasters, tragedies.

I am a poet of the high seas,
The captain and the crew,
A free man of free passage,
So all others can join me.

Healing Gila

for The People

The people don't mention it much.
It goes without saying,
it stays without saying—

that concentration camp
on their reservation.

And they avoid that massive site
as they avoid contamination—

that massive void
punctuated by crusted nails,
punctured pipes, crumbled
failings of foundations . . .

What else is there to say?

This was a lush land once,
graced by a gifted people
gifted with the wisdom
of rivers, seasons, irrigation.

The waters went flowing
through a network of canals
in the delicate workings
of balances and health . . .

What else is there to say?

Then came the nation.
Then came the death.

Then came the desert.
Then came the camp.

But the desert is not deserted.
It goes without saying,
it stays without saying—

wind, spirits, tumbleweeds, pain.

Children of Camp

As performed with Pat Suzuki and George Takei—
"Triumph of the Human Spirit," Sacramento, 1997

I.

Actor.   Singer.   Poet.
Children of Camp.

Actor.   Singer.   Poet.
Children of dreams.

Actor.   Singer.   Poet.
Children of history.

II.

My parents taught me
how to act.
My parents taught me
by their own example.

From my parents
I learned to act
with dignity.
From my parents
I learned to act
with strength.

In the confines of camp
the roles were many.
I was dutiful son.
I was helpful friend.
I was respectful neighbor.

In the confines of camp
the scenes were many.
There was the daily drama
of the mess halls.
There was the daily drama
of the latrines.
There was the daily drama
of human interaction.

We were a cast of thousands
on the stage of confinement,
expressing the full range
of our considerable lives:
sorrow, fear, anger, joy . . .

From my parents
I learned how to act.
From my parents
I learned how to survive.

When I look back
at my acting career,
I give thanks
to my mother and my father.

III.

My singing came to me
as a gift from my mother.
She sang me to sleep
in the peaceful nights,
she sang me to wake
in the glorious mornings.

I grew up singing.
I grew up voicing
the joys of life
in the sunny fields
of our California home.

I sang the songs
of the radio.
I sang the songs
of America.
I sang the songs
of freedom—

of blossoms and birds,
of holidays and festivals,
of what it means
to enjoy being a girl.

But in the confines of camp
that girl could not sing.
But in the confines of camp
that girl fell into silence.

She lost her voice.
She had no songs to sing.

But her mother said:
"Come, child.
come sing with me.
Come, child.
Let us make music together.
Come, child.
Let us sing of beauty.
Come, child.
Let us sing of love.
Come, child.
Let us sing for the better."

And the girl and her mother
became a melody.
And the girl and her mother
became a harmony.
And the girl and her mother
became a song of power.

And that song
is stronger
than barbed wire.

IV.

There was no poetry in camp.
Unless you can say
mud is poetry,
unless you can say
dust is poetry,
unless you can say
blood is poetry,
unless you can say
cruelty is poetry,
unless you can say
injustice is poetry,
unless you can say
imprisonment is poetry.

There was no poetry in camp.
Unless you can say
families are poetry,
unless you can say
people are poetry.

And the people
made poetry

from camp.
And the people
made poetry
in camp.

The people made poetry
with their very own hands—
little gifts from scrap
for precious loved ones,
friends, elders, children.

And the people made poetry
with their very own vision—
ways of seeing beauty,
ways of seeing humor,
ways of seeing nature.

And the people made poetry
with their very own hearts—
ways of feeling community,
ways of feeling spirit,
ways of feeling appreciation.

There was no poetry in camp.
But the people made it so.
With hands, vision, hearts,
the people made it so.

v.

Actors.   Singers.   Poets.
Our people of camp.

Actors.   Singers.   Poets.
Our people of humanity.

Scanning the Century

I. BLUES

In actuality,
shades of gray.

Think: "X-ray."

II. LOUIS "POPS" ARMSTRONG

Put it this way,
without explanation:

Pops put the "pop!"
into this carbon

nation.

III. EDWARD KENNEDY "DUKE" ELLINGTON

Duke, with his elegant manner,
and his unanimous stature
as a monumental composer
of and to and for his community,

was commissioned to compose,
by the people themselves,
inspiring anthems for national
monuments and memorials;

that way, each site would
resonate with a familiar ring
through the visionary melodies

of the acknowledged master . . .
So Duke, in all benevolence,
set out to do just that—
with his initial objective
being hallowed Mount Rushmore.

There, Duke arrived in style,
as a statesman, in a composed
state of mind, like a pilgrim,
but instead of being his usual

expansive, expressive self,
Duke, mysteriously, fell mute,
and instead of musical notes,
snow fell onto his paper . . .

And Duke just fell to his knees
in that congested parking lot.
And Duke just stared back
at those crags, at that

recognizable rock, and cried
out loud like his mother's child.

IV. WILLIAM "COUNT" BASIE

Counts don't count
in this country.
Count knew that.

But Count could count.
Count could figure.
Count snapped his fingers

and calculated the total
rhythm by which we function
to this very day. In sum:

———————————

Hey, notice how the Count
has you tapping your feet
as he counts off the beat

to the Basic, swinging,
snappy figures of your
Social Security Number.

V. LESTER WILLIS "PRES" YOUNG

Presidential—that's him.
That's why you elected him.
That's why you return him
to office, term after term . . .

That's why, year after year,
you send him a note of thanks
each blooming April—
perennially grateful

for his Executive Action—
because this is The Man
who, with a stroke
of a note, pres

ented *you* with your *personal*
Internal
Revenue
Service.

VI. BILLIE "LADY DAY" HOLIDAY

Think: "Female."
Think: "Daily."

VII. CHARLIE "BIRD" PARKER

In each tune,
Bird begins with
a hearty "hello"
to engage you

in a heartfelt
conversation
concluding with
a gracious "goodbye"

which leaves you
all the better
and never quite
alone.

What Bird shows
on the saxophone
is how to blow
on the telephone.

VIII. JOHN BIRKS "DIZZY" GILLESPIE

Despite his moniker,
Dizzy, actually,
was a healer,
and his music
is the feeling
following dizziness.

IX. THELONIOUS MONK

Even if you've never heard his music,
you've undoubtedly seen him—

the man going around old neighborhoods
in a hat and coat,

a friendly man, with a ready smile,
who just doesn't say much.

We take him for granted
as he goes about his business

shifting leaves with his foot,
occasionally picking up something

for inspection, examining the gravel
or just plain dirt around churches.

When he gets home, he empties his pockets.
Bent, broken, discarded—

to him, they're not worthless.
Instead, he blows on them,

strokes them, holds them up to the light,
and plants them in his old piano.

Hard to imagine, but those old notes,
when he summons them, rise up and shine!

X. EARL "BUD" POWELL

Except for occasional
flashes of brilliance,
Bud was a failure—

out of work,
out of favor
in his nation.

As a result,
his legacy
is recognized

only upon occasion
during one night
in early July.

XI. MILES DEWEY DAVIS III

Three fingers of the right hand—
those are the ones he used

to measure his music,
measure upon measure,

and, certainly, he measured
by Miles, for he was the third.

The fourth was the future,
significant of those to come . . .

And the past, of course, played
a part in his sound: the thumb.

XII. JOHN WILLIAM COLTRANE

Looking back from the lofty confines
of the late twentieth century,
through the darkness of clouds,
the shifting shadows,
the violent storms,

you see a light form,
you hear a hymn.

That's him.

PICKING UP STONES

Nyogen Senzaki, the erstwhile Zen teacher
(he had no degrees, didn't call himself "master"),
while interned in Wyoming
(he didn't call himself "internee" either),

went about gathering pebbles
and writing words on them—
common words, in Japanese
with a brush dipped in ink.

Then he'd return them
to their source, as best he could,
the ink would wash,
and no harm was done.

However, several residents, likewise
elderly with nothing better to do,
observed his practice
and set about collecting
the Sensei's stones.

It became a kind of game
to pass the time,
to seek and find—
like an "Eastern eggless hunt."

And even in the confines of camp,
possibilities were endless—

for Senzaki, without having to resort
to trickery, would simply
scatter his gathering,

and it was difficult to tell
which was which:

"his" pebbles, just plain pebbles,
or those which, in his hands,
had remained mute,
dictating silence . . .

And it was an amusing sight
to see these old people
shuffling about in dust,
mud, snow, sleet—
sometimes even crushing
ice with their feet—

with their eyes to the ground,
bent on pursuing the old man's path,
giving everything close inspection,
pausing occasionally
to smile, exclaim, even laugh,

and essentially going around
putting rocks in their pockets . . .

Still, as they put it,
this place was perfect for pebbles,
so rich with rounded stones,
some of which reflected
the colorful proximity of Yellowstone
itself, likewise ministered
by their government;

moreover, pebble-searching
had resulted in enlightening
arrowhead finds,

inspiring some elders
to try their hand
at chipping obsidian
in this land
where the buffalo roamed . . .

Eventually, in respectable homes,
some of those stones
assumed resting places
on special mantels and shelves—

worthless souvenirs, certainly,
of only sentimental value,
for although the rocks
may speak to some
of distant days,
of generations past,
like mini-milestones,

they're still just anonymous rocks
with faded words on them:
MAKE   TEACHING   HOUSE   SCENT
GREED   YOUNG   SEED   LEAVE
NOTHING   EVERYTHING   CHANGE   EAST
PRAY   PARENTS   UNIVERSE   SHINE
LISTEN   RESPECT   KNOWLEDGE   MIND . . .

And as for Senzaki,
he died in obscurity,
an old dishwasher
with few friends,

resting, perhaps,
among headstones
in Los Angeles,

a citi-Zen, of sorts,
of the earth,

one who spoke
broken English

and wrote
on some stones

WHILE   LEAVING   OTHERS   ALONE.

Drawing the Line

For Yosh Kuromiya

I.

Yosh is drawing the line.
It's a good line, on paper,
and a good morning
for just such an endeavor—

and the line seems to find
its own way, flowing
across the white expanse

like a dark, new river . . .

II.

Yes, Yosh is drawing the line.
And you might say he's simply
following his own nature—

he's always had a good eye,
a fine sense of perspective,
and a sure hand, a gift

for making things ring true,
and come clearer into view.

III.

So the line makes its way,
on paper, charting a clear
course like a signature,

starting from the left
and toward the bottom end,
logically and gradually
and gracefully ascending

to the center, where it takes
a sharp turn upward, straight
toward the top before it
finds itself leveling off
to the right again, descending

slightly for a while before
dropping straight down, coming
to a rest near the bottom,

bending, descending gradually
and gracefully as it began, but

at the other side of the space . . .

IV.

No sooner said than done.
Yosh relaxes for the moment,
blinks his eyes, realizing

his intensity of focus, almost
like prayer, a sunrise meditation.

V.

Ah, another beautiful morning!
Time to move on, see what the day
provides by way of promise . . .

And as for the drawing, well,
the line is drawn, on paper—

other dimensions can come later . . .

VI.

Yosh, although a young man,
a teenager, is naturally
calm and confident by nature.

Thus, when he draws a line,
it tends to stay drawn.
He may make adjustments
but doesn't make mistakes.

That's just the way he is—
trusting his own judgement
as a person, as an artist.

As a result, he is a most
trusted friend, judging
from the many friends who
count on him, rely on him,
respect what he has to say . . .

That's just the way he is—
good-hearted, as they say:
"If you need a favor, ask
Yosh; he'll go out of his way . . ."

VII.

Still, though, you've got to draw the line
somewhere—and as the saying goes,

so goes Yosh. And his friends know
certain things not to ask of him.

What "everybody does" just may not go
with Yosh, the set of beliefs, the sense
of integrity, values, he got from his folks.

VIII.

As for this drawing in his sketchbook,
you might well ask: "What is it?"

At this stage, it's just a line—
a line that goes sideways, up, over,
down, descending to the other margin.

Is it just a line? An abstract design?
Or might it stand for something?

At first glance, it looks to be a line
charting the progress of something
that goes along slowly, rising
a bit to indicate, oh, maybe a normal
growth rate or business-as-usual,

when all of a sudden it jumps, reflecting
a decisive turn of events which lasts
a while before resuming

what might be assumed to be a more
regular course of activity concluding

at what may represent the present
on the journey from the then to the now . . .

That's what graphs show, the flow
of activity, the rise and fall of events
often out of our hands, so it can become
gratifying to simply resume the bottom
line of normalcy again, starting over
at square one, back to the drawing board . . .

That is, it could have been worse.
The line could have been broken, snapped,
or bottomed out into nothing, going
nowhere fast like the slow and steady
line monitoring a silent patient . . .

Or, the line could have turned back
into itself into a dead-end maze,
a meaningless mass of angles and tangles . . .

Ah, but if you asked an observant child,
the answer might be: "Well, it just looks
like the bottom of my baby sister's mouth—
'cause when she smiles, she only has one tooth!"

And if you asked Yosh, he'd simply say,
in his modest way: "Oh, that's just Heart Mountain."

IX.

Maybe you had to be there.
For if you were, you would not only
not have to ask, but you would
appreciate the profile, the likeness

of what looms large in your life
and mind, as large as life staring
you in the face day by day by day

and so on into night, where it is so
implanted in your sight and mind
that the ancient promontory assumes
a prominence in your mildest dreams,
and even when the dust billows, or clouds
cover it, blowing snow and sleet and rain,

you can't avoid it, you can count on it,
Heart Mountain. Heart Mountain
is still there. And you're here.

X.

Ah, but it is, after all,
just a mountain—one of many,
actually, in this region,
in this range, and if anything
distinguishes it, it's just
its individual shape and name.

And the fact that it stands
rising up out of the plains
so close you can touch it,
you can almost but not quite

get there on a Sunday picnic,
your voices echoing in the ever-
green forest on its slopes . . .

As it stands, it is a remote
monument to, a testament to
something that stands to be
respected from a distance,

accessible only in dreams,
those airy, carefree moments
before the truth comes crashing
home to your home in the camp . . .

XI.

Yosh can take you there, though,
by drawing the line, on paper.

And Yosh, with his own given name,
is somewhat like the mountain—

an individual, certainly, but also
rather common to this region.
He's just so-and-so's kid,
or just another regular teenager
engaged in whatever it takes these days . . .

But this morning, it was different.
He was out there at the crack of dawn,
pacing around over by the fence,
blowing into his hands, rubbing
his hands, slapping, clapping
his hands together as if in preparation

to undertake something special
instead of doing the nothing he did—

that is, he just got to his knees
and knelt there, facing the mountain.

Knelt there. Knelt there. Is he praying?
But now he's writing. But writing what?

Then, as sunlight struck the mountain,
and the ordinary idle elder
and the regular bored child
approached Yosh, they could tell
from the size of the wide sketchpad
that he was drawing—but drawing
what? Well, that's obvious—but what for?

XII.

Seeing the drawing was its own reward.
Boy, look at that! He's got it right!
You've got to admire him for that.

And, boy, if you really look at it—
in this sunrise light, under this
wide, blue sky—why, it really is
a beautiful sight, that majestic
hunk of rock they call Heart Mountain.

And to top it off, this talented guy
sure accentuates the positive, because
he *didn't* include the posts and wire.

XIII.

Yosh, smiling, greeting, is striding
toward the barracks. There's a line
at the mess hall, a line at the toilets.

Better check in with the folks. Mom's
all right, but Dad's never adjusted.
I may or may not show him the drawing.

It depends. He likes me to stay active,
but this might be the wrong subject.
It might rub him wrong, get him
in a mountain-mood of reminiscing
about California, the mountains of home.

And, heck, those were just hills
by comparison, but they've taken on
size in his eyes; still, when I fill in
the shading, the forest, tonight, maybe
he can appreciate it for just what it is:

Heart Mountain, in Wyoming, a drawing
by his dutiful son here with the family
doing its duties—kitchen duty, latrine duty . . .

I'll do my duties; and I've got my own duty, my
right, to do what I can, to see this through . . .

XIV.

The sketchbook drops to the cot.
Brrr, better go get some coal.
It's the least I can do—not worth
much else, me, without a real line

of work. But this art might get me
someplace—maybe even a career
in here. Doing portraits of inmates.

But out there is *in here* too, related—
it's a matter of perspective, like lines
of lineage and history, like the line
between me and the fencepost, between

me and the flagpole, between stars,
stripes, the searchlight, and the guy
on duty in the guardtower, maybe
like me, from California, looking
up at the airplane making a line
of sound in the sky, searching
for the right place in a time of peace . . .

Yes, if I had a big enough piece
of paper, I'd draw the line
tracing the way we came, smooth
as tracks clear back to California,

and in the other direction, the line
clean out to the city of Philadelphia
and the Liberty Bell ringing testimony
over Independence Hall and the framing
of the Constitution. Yes, it's there,
and I can see it, in the right frame of mind . . .

xv.

No, you have no right
to imprison my parents.

No, you have no right
to deny us our liberty.

Yes, I have my right
to stand for our justice.

Yes, I have my right
to stand for our freedom.

xvi.

And this is where Yosh
drew the line—

on paper, on the pages
of the Constitution.

xvii.

The rest is history.
Arrested, judged,
sentenced, imprisoned

for two years
for refusing
induction under

such conditions:
"as long as my
family is in here . . ."

Eventually arrives
a few sentences
of presidential

pardon, period.
But history
doesn't rest,

as Yosh gives
testimony,
drawing the line,
on paper, again.

XVIII.

This time, though, he's a free man
with a free mind and a very clear
conscience, having come full circle
to this clear spring at Heart Mountain.

And Heart Mountain, of course,
is still here, timeless and ever-
changing in the seasons, the light,
standing, withstanding the test of time.

And this time Yosh is free to roam
his home range like an antelope,
circling the mountain, seeing all sides
with new visions, wide perspectives:

from here, it comes to a narrow peak;
from here, it presents the profile
of a cherished parent, strong, serene;
from here, yes, it could be a tooth;
and from anywhere, forever, a heart.

Yes, that's about the truth of it—
once a heart, always a heart—

a monumental testament under the sky.

This time, though, Yosh is strolling
over a freshly plowed and fenceless field
with that very same sketchbook, searching
through the decades to find that rightful
place in relation to the mountain, wanting
to show his wife where the drawing happened,

where that quiet young man sank to his knees
in reverence for the mountain, in silent
celebration for that vision of beauty
that evoked such wonder, such a sunrise
of inspiration, wisdom, and compassion

that the line drew itself, making its way
with conviction in the direction it knew
to be right across the space, on paper,

and yes, yes, the heart, the eye, the mind
testify this is right, here, Yosh, hold
up the drawing, behold the mountain, trust
the judgement upholding truth through time
as the man, the mountain, the profile make
a perfect fit in this right place and time
for Yosh to kneel again, feel again, raise
his radiant eyes in peace to face the radiant
mountain, Heart Mountain, Heart Mountain—

and begin, again, with confidence, to draw the line!